Smoking

Dr. Alvin Silverstein,

Virginia Silverstein, and

Laura Silverstein Nunn

My Health
Franklin Watts

A Division of Scholastic Inc.

New York • Toronto • London • Auckland • Sydney

Mexico City • New Delhi • Hong Kong

Danbury, Connecticut

Photographs © 2003: Corbis Images: 18 (Lester V. Bergman), 25 (Duomo); Custom Medical Stock Photo: 23, 24; Photo Researchers, NY: 26 (John Bavosi), 9 (BSIP/Eristiot), 27 (Mark Clarke), 14 (Gilbert S. Grant), 13 (Damien Lovegrove), 21 (Doug Martin), 29 (Richard T. Nowitz), 28 (Blair Seitz), 36 (Jim Selby), 19 top (SIU), 19 bottom (James Steveson), 34 (Sheila Terry); PhotoEdit: 38 (Myrleen Cate), 7 (Mary Kate Denny), 20 (Tony Freeman), 40 (Jeff Greenberg), 4, 6 (Michael Newman) 22, 31 (David Young-Wolff); Visuals Unlimited: 10 (Veronika Burmeister), 15 (Jeff J. Daly), 17 (Jeff Greenberg).

Cartoons by Rick Stromoski

Library of Congress Cataloging-in-Publication Data

Silverstein, Alvin.
    Smoking / by Dr. Alvin Silverstein, Virginia Silverstein, and Laura Silverstein Nunn.
        p. (cm.)—(My Health)
    Includes bibliographical references and index.
    Contents: Smoking stinks! — Your heart and lungs — What's in a cigarette? — What's wrong with smoking? — Why do people smoke? — It's quitting time.
    ISBN 0-531-12193-9 (lib. bdg.)   0-531-16239-7 (pbk.)
    1. Smoking—Juvenile literature. [1. Smoking.] I. Silverstein, Virginia B. II. Nunn, Laura Silverstein. III. Title. IV. Series.
RC567.S56 2003
616.86′5—dc21   2002001729

C●ntents

Smoking Stinks!

Have you ever been around people who smoke cigarettes? You can usually tell when people have been smoking by the way they smell. Even when they are not smoking, a smoky smell stays in their clothing and hair. Smoking also causes lasting effects inside the body.

Cigarette smoke contains chemicals that can damage important organs, such as the lungs and heart. Smokers may have trouble catching their breath while doing everyday activities, such as climbing stairs or playing sports. After years of smoking, more serious health problems may develop. For example, smoking can lead to a heart attack or lung cancer, which can kill. More than 400,000 Americans die each year from health problems related to cigarette smoking.

Did You Know...

In the United States, more than 4 million teenagers between the ages of thirteen and seventeen and 100,000 children under age thirteen smoke cigarettes.

◀ People who smoke cigarettes often smell like stale smoke.

5

Many smokers are aware of the dangers, but they still continue to smoke. Why? Part of the reason is habit—it is part of their daily routine. But even if they want to quit smoking, they may not be able to. Cigarettes contain a drug that, after a while, fools the smokers' bodies into thinking they need the drug to feel "right." Without it, they start to feel jittery, anxious, and irritable. Those feelings go away once they light up another cigarette. But with some help, smokers can eventually quit for good.

Smoking is also harmful to nonsmokers who happen to breathe in cigarette smoke. This is why many public places, such as hospitals, restaurants, and shopping centers, are now smoke-free or have special smoking areas.

Many restaurants do not permit smoking.

The Heart and Lungs

Every single day you take thousands of breaths, and most of the time you don't even realize it. Breathing is automatic—we do it without thinking about it. But you do notice your breathing when you're running around at soccer practice or gasping for air in a room filled with cigarette smoke.

When you breathe in, or *inhale*, you bring in air through your nose and mouth. Then the air passes down into your *lungs*. These two large, spongy organs in your chest fill up with air and expand, like balloons. Air contains oxygen, an invisible gas that we need to live. Your body uses oxygen to produce

Some activities, such as exercise, make you notice your breathing.

7

the energy you need for things like running, playing, thinking, eating, and even sleeping. Oxygen passes from the lungs into the blood, which carries this gas to the cells of the body.

When body cells use oxygen to produce energy, they make a gas called carbon dioxide as a waste product. The blood carries carbon dioxide to the lungs, where it is pushed out when you breathe out, or **exhale**. Then the process starts all over again, and the lungs bring in fresh air.

Both smoking and being around cigarette smoke can damage the lungs. Lung damage makes it hard to breathe normally. To understand how this happens, take a closer look at your breathing system, called the **respiratory system**.

The respiratory system looks a lot like an upside-down tree. The air you breathe goes down your throat, called the **pharynx**, and continues through the main breathing tube, or **trachea**.

X RAY

You can feel the trachea at the front of your throat. At the end of the trachea are two large tubes called **bronchi**, which lead into the right and left lungs. The bronchi branch into thinner tubes, called **bronchioles**, which look like the branches of a tree.

The bronchioles lead into millions of tiny, balloonlike air bags in the lungs called **alveoli**. They look like tiny bunches of grapes, but they are too small to see without a microscope. The walls of the alveoli are so thin that gases can pass right through them. Many tiny tubes called **blood vessels** form nets that wrap around each of the alveoli. These blood vessels have very thin walls, which allow oxygen to move easily out of the alveoli into the blood, and carbon dioxide to pass easily from the blood into the alveoli.

Trachea

Bronchi

Lungs

Bronchioles

All the parts of the respiratory system work together to make breathing easy.

9

The airways have defenses that protect the lungs from dust, germs, and other solid particles that may be breathed in from the air. Some particles that enter your nose get trapped in bristly hairs inside your nostrils. Other particles fall into a gooey fluid called **mucus**, which covers the lining of your nose. Mucus is also produced in the airways and traps any pollen grains and tiny bits of dust that might have gotten through. Tiny, hairlike **cilia** in the lining of the breathing tubes move back and forth. The cilia are too small to see without a microscope, but their

Bristly cilia in the breathing tubes move dust away from the lungs.

movements make waves in the mucus. The waves help to sweep trapped particles up and away from your lungs. The particles leave your body when you blow your nose, sneeze, or cough.

The lungs work together with the heart to send oxygen and food chemicals to your body cells. Your heart is a pump that sends blood rushing through blood vessels to bring food and oxygen to your body's cells. Blood also carries away the cells' waste products.

The heart is actually a **muscle**. Like any muscle, the heart contracts, or tightens, and then relaxes. Before each contraction, the heart fills with blood. Blood from all over your body flows into the right side of the heart, while oxygen-rich blood from the lungs flows into the left side. Then, when the heart **contracts**, the right side sends blood to the lungs to get a new supply of oxygen. The left side pumps the oxygen-rich blood from the lungs into a big blood vessel whose branches lead to all parts of the body.

Did You Know....

It takes about fifteen minutes for a particle to be carried out of the airways.

Tik Tik Tik Tik

Activity 1: How Fast Do You Breathe?

When you are breathing quietly, you inhale and exhale between ten and fourteen times a minute. When you exercise, run, or dance, your body needs more oxygen to produce more energy. You need to breathe faster and deeper so your lungs can take in more oxygen. When you are very active, the cells in the body use up oxygen from the blood faster than it can be replaced, and you feel "out of breath."

In this activity, you can find out how many breaths you take at rest and how many breaths you take during and after exercise. You need a watch with a second hand, paper, and a pencil. Count how many breaths you take in one minute while you are sitting. Write down that number and label it "sitting." Then run in place for two minutes. Count the number of breaths you take during the second minute that you are running, and then count them for a minute right after you stop running. Write down the number for "running" and the number for "after running." Now compare the three numbers. What differences do you notice?

What's in a Cigarette?

A cigarette looks like a white stick with a dark center. The white wrapper is made of thin paper, which covers tightly rolled dried leaves from *tobacco* plants. Tobacco contains chemicals that can produce various effects on the body.

A cigarette is made up of dried tobacco leaves rolled up in thin paper.

How do tobacco chemicals get into the body? People usually take in tobacco chemicals by smoking tobacco leaves. The tobacco is burned, and the smoke and hot gases are drawn into the lungs. Chemicals in the smoke pass through the linings of the nose, mouth, throat, and lungs. Some of them pass into the blood and are carried throughout the body.

Plant Poisons

Some plants produce bitter-tasting, often poisonous chemicals to protect themselves from danger. The bitter taste is a warning that these chemicals may be harmful. A caterpillar or snail that tastes a leaf will not want to eat any more—so a bitter taste can save its life. Tobacco belongs to this group of poisonous plants. Humans, however, sometimes ignore nature's warnings. Instead of avoiding tobacco, many people seek out its bitter taste and even learn to enjoy it.

Tobacco plants

Cigarettes, cigars, and pipe tobacco are all forms of tobacco that are smoked. There are also some forms of "smokeless tobacco" that are not burned. Chewing tobacco is tucked inside a person's cheek or under the tongue. Chemicals in the tobacco pass into the saliva and then through the lining of the mouth and into the blood. Snuff is tobacco in a fine powdered form, which is sniffed into the nose. The chemicals get into the blood through the lining of the nose.

One of the most important chemicals in tobacco is **nicotine**. Nicotine is a powerful drug that acts on the heart and blood vessels, making the heart pump faster and harder. It can speed up the breathing rate. It also affects the brain. Nicotine reaches the brain only eight seconds after a person inhales

Smokeless tobacco is another way that people get nicotine.

15

tobacco smoke. Inside the brain, nicotine acts like one of the body's own signal chemicals, which help brain cells send messages to each other. Small doses of nicotine can make it easier to concentrate, learn, and remember. Nicotine also acts on parts of the brain that produce feelings of pleasure and satisfaction. It can make a person feel relaxed.

The "feel-good" effect of nicotine is an important part of why it is so hard to stop smoking. People get used to reaching for a cigarette whenever they feel tense or upset, because the drug in the smoke helps them to feel calmer. Smoking becomes part of their daily routine—a cigarette after each meal, for example, and more cigarettes when they need to concentrate on solving a hard problem. Habits are hard to break, but that is not the whole reason why it's hard to stop.

Scientists have found that nicotine is **addictive**. That means nicotine produces chemical changes in the brain that make the brain need more doses of the drug just to feel normal.

Did You Know...

Nicotine is so poisonous that farmers use it to kill insects.

Remember that nicotine acts like one of the brain's own signal chemicals and produces feelings of pleasure. If a person stops smoking, there are not as many signal chemicals around, and the brain's pleasure centers do not get as many messages. So the person begins to feel restless and irritable, hungry, headachy, and depressed. These feelings are actually **withdrawal symptoms** caused by the lack of the drug that the brain has become used to. So the smoker feels the need to light up another cigarette.

What's Wrong With Smoking?

Picture this—your clothes and hair stink of cigarette smoke. Your breath smells so bad that people do not want to get close to you. Your teeth are yellow. Your fingers have brown stains from tobacco. Foods don't smell and taste as good as they used to. That's what it's like to be a smoker. But that's only how it affects you on the surface.

Cigarette smoke contains more than four thousand different chemicals. When tobacco is burned, the

Yellow teeth and bad breath are two side effects of smoking.

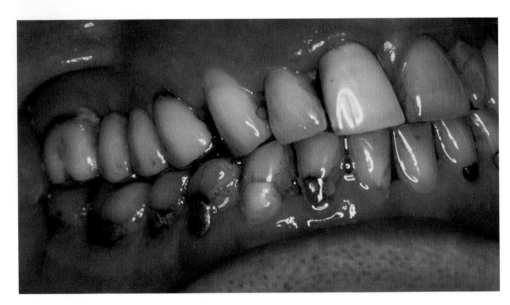

temperature inside the cigarette can go as high as 2,000°F (1,093°C). This tremendous heat breaks down the tobacco and produces chemicals such as the poisonous gas carbon monoxide. This gas is picked up by the red blood cells that normally carry oxygen. The red blood cells hold it so tightly that they can't let go, so they can no longer carry oxygen. As a result, the body cells do not get as much oxygen as they need, and the smoker may be short of breath.

Cigarette smoke also contains tar, a complicated mixture of gummy chemicals that sticks to the airways and settles in the lungs. In fact, the lungs of a longtime smoker look black instead of a healthy pink. The tar is what stains the smoker's fingers and teeth. It produces bad breath and dulls the senses of taste and smell. Because foods don't taste as good, smokers may lose their appetites. Some of the many chemicals in the tar can damage cells and cause cancer.

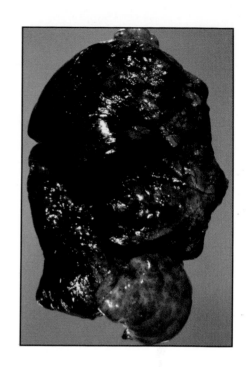

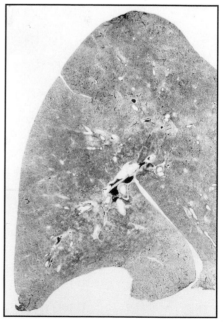

Compare the color of the smoker's lung (top) with the healthy lung (bottom).

Smokeless Is Not Harmless

"Smokeless" tobacco does not have tar and won't cause lung cancer, but it isn't harmless. Chewing tobacco can cause gum disease and cancer of the mouth, and the nicotine it contains can lead to heart disease. In fact, chewing tobacco can deliver an even higher dose of nicotine to the user than smoking can. And like smoking cigarettes, chewing tobacco is very addictive.

Smokeless tobacco

Some harmful effects of smoking may develop just weeks after a person starts smoking regularly. Smoking harms the respiratory organs in a number of ways. First, the smoker draws in hot gases with each puff. These gases are so hot that they burn the delicate cells that line the nose, throat, and airways. They damage the cilia on the surface of these cells, stopping them from sweeping out dust and other solid particles. A single cigarette slows down the movement of the cilia, and heavy smoking destroys them completely. As a result, mucus builds up, and the smoker has to work extra hard to cough the gunk out. In fact, coughing is so common among smokers that the ailment is often called "smoker's cough."

Damage to the cells lining the airways also allows germs to get inside the body more easily. Smokers tend to get more colds and other respiratory illnesses than people who don't smoke.

As a person continues to smoke, more serious respiratory problems may develop. Damage to the airways causes **inflammation** (redness and swelling). This is a condition known as **bronchitis**. The space inside the bronchi becomes narrow, and it gets harder to breathe. Mucus builds up and the smoker continually coughs, trying to bring it up through the narrowed airways. Smokers are six times more likely to get bronchitis than are nonsmokers.

Smokers frequently cough to clear the extra mucus from their throats.

Secondhand Smoke

When a cigarette smoker takes a puff and then exhales, chemicals from the burning tobacco are sent out into the air. Not only does the smoker breathe in these poisons, but everyone around that person does too. So if you don't smoke but spend time near someone who does, you are breathing in **secondhand smoke**. Inhaling somebody else's smoke can give you the same kinds of health problems that smokers develop. Studies have found that kids who live with a parent who smokes have more respiratory problems, such as colds or bronchitis, than those who live in a smoke-free household. Secondhand smoke also acts as a **trigger** for people with **asthma**, a disease that causes the airways to become narrow. So being around someone who smokes can bring on asthma symptoms more often and even make them worse.

Parents who smoke should never expose their children to the dangerous fumes.

Eventually, as a person continues smoking, the alveoli in the lungs may become damaged and stop working normally. The lungs become less elastic (stretchable) and can't hold as much air. This is a serious lung condition called **emphysema**. For someone with emphysema, every breath is a struggle. Nonsmokers

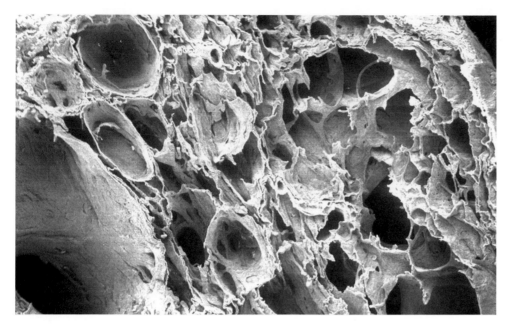

Emphysema is a condition that destroys the lungs.

use about 5 percent of their energy for breathing, but people with emphysema may use as much as 80 percent of their energy just to get air into and out of their lungs. They may need to breathe pure oxygen from an oxygen tank to get all that they need.

More than forty chemicals in the tar in tobacco smoke are known to cause cancer. Cancer develops when damaged cells go out of control and begin to multiply wildly. They build up into solid lumps, called **tumors**. Cancer cells steal food from healthy body cells. They push their way into healthy tissues and choke out the normal cells. They can cause a lot of damage in an organ and can spread to other parts

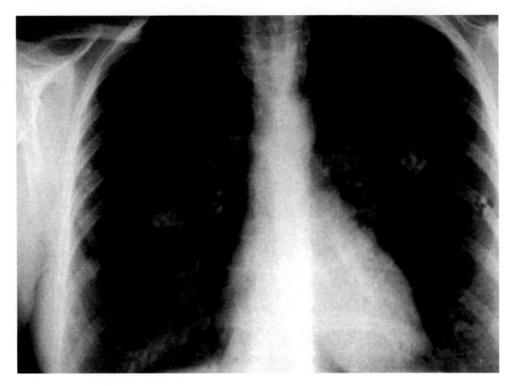

The red blotches in this x-ray indicate that the patient has lung cancer.

of the body. Eventually, they can kill a person. Lung cancer is one of the major killers of people who smoke. Smokers may also develop cancer of the mouth, throat, and even organs such as the kidneys and bladder.

While tar does the most harm to the lungs, nicotine has serious effects on the heart and blood vessels. When nicotine gets into the blood, it causes the blood vessels to **constrict** (narrow). The heart then has to work harder to pump blood through the body. Eventually, the heart may become weakened because of the extra strain put on it for such a long period of time. These kinds of problems do not usually occur unless a person has smoked for many years, but smoking at a young age can lead to serious heart conditions later in life.

Smokers Don't Make Good Athletes

You know that smoking can have serious effects on a person's breathing ability. So can you imagine what happens to an athlete who smokes? The body uses a lot of oxygen to produce energy that fuels sports activities. When a person exercises regularly, the heart becomes stronger and bigger and, therefore, can pump more blood in each heartbeat. It provides enough oxygen to muscles without working too hard. So a trained athlete usually has a slower heart rate than a person who doesn't exercise. When an athlete smokes, however, nicotine increases the heart rate, but instead of bringing in more oxygen, the blood carries less oxygen

Smoking will hurt your athletic performance.

because of the carbon monoxide in the cigarette smoke. Therefore, athletes who smoke cannot get enough oxygen to produce the energy their bodies need to move.

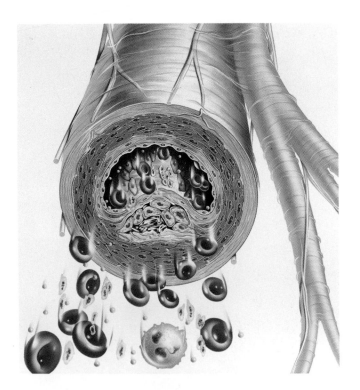

The heart is a hardworking organ that needs plenty of oxygen. Because smoking adds carbon monoxide to the blood, there are fewer red blood cells available to carry oxygen. When the heart doesn't get all the oxygen it needs, it may become damaged. Carbon monoxide also causes a fatty substance called **cholesterol** to build up inside a person's **arteries**. (Arteries are the blood vessels that carry blood from the heart to other parts of the body.) Eventually, the arteries become so clogged with fatty material that the blood flow to the heart is greatly reduced or even cut off. This can lead to a heart attack.

When arteries are clogged, the narrow opening may be closed off completely by a **blood clot**. Blood clots are useful when you have a cut. Tiny blood cells called **platelets** become sticky when they run into the edges of a damaged blood vessel. They start to pile up until they form a plug that fills the hole. They may also break open and spill out chemicals that cause blood to thicken into a net of fibers that help to patch the hole and stop the bleeding. The chemicals in cigarette smoke make the platelets especially sticky, so a clot may form even where there isn't a cut. When a blood clot plugs up an artery carrying blood to the heart, the heart can't get enough oxygen and its muscle cells may die. This can cause a heart attack. If a blood clot occurs in a blood vessel that leads to the brain, the oxygen supply to the brain is cut off and brain cells may die. This results in a **stroke**, a serious condition in which a person may lose the ability to speak or move a body part.

More Bad Things About Smoking

Smokers are more likely to have:
- Accidents and injuries
- Arthritis (stiff joints)
- Backaches
- Baldness
- Gum disease
- Hearing problems
- Mood swings
- Slower healing of injuries
- Stomach problems
- Weakened bones
- Wrinkled skin

Smoking is one cause of wrinkled skin.

Why Do People Smoke?

"Everybody's doing it!" That's what many teenagers think when they see their friends or other kids light up a cigarette after school or at a party. Although the number of teenage smokers is growing, smoking is not as common as many kids think. But kids who

Saying no to cigarettes now will prevent serious smoking-related health problems later in life.

think that everyone's doing it are more likely to start smoking themselves.

It's not easy being a teenager. Many teens worry about fitting in or being "cool." They might feel that if they smoked, they would have something in common with other kids who smoke. Then they could finally be one of the "cool" kids. Smoking also helps kids get through stressful times. Remember that the chemicals in cigarette smoke reach pleasure centers in the brain,

How Many Teens Smoke?

Every day, more than 3,000 American teenagers become regular smokers. That's 1 million kids every year. By age thirteen, about 56 percent of American kids have tried smoking and 9 percent have become regular smokers. By age seventeen, as many as 77 percent of American teenagers have tried smoking, but only 25 percent of all teens have become regular smokers. Does 25 percent sound like everybody's doing it?

Sometimes it can be hard to say no to cigarettes when your friends smoke.

so people tend to reach for a cigarette when they are upset or worried about something.

Sometimes teenage smokers tease nonsmokers who don't want to try cigarettes. If someone asked you if you wanted a cigarette, what would you say? It's really hard to say no when your friends are making you feel bad for not smoking. But it's up to you—if you don't take those first puffs now, you won't get hooked. Imagine how much trouble you will save yourself later on.

Many teenage smokers probably don't think that advertising has anything to do with why they smoke, but many health experts would disagree. People often want to buy things that they see advertised on television and radio, or in magazines and newspapers. Many times they don't even realize why they suddenly want a new kind of cereal or the latest video game. The same thing happens when people see a colorful magazine ad showing people smoking and having fun. It looks like smoking is part of being grown-up and having a good time.

Did You Know...

You are more likely to start smoking if you have friends or parents who smoke.

Tobacco companies are no longer allowed to advertise cigarettes or other tobacco products on television. They can make their point in a different way, though. Each time you see a character smoking in a movie or on a television show, you get the message that smoking is a normal thing to do. Seeing baseball players chewing tobacco and spitting it on the field makes it look like smokeless tobacco is harmless and cool.

Some people say that tobacco companies are aiming their ads at kids. The companies claim that they are not, and never did—yet they used to use popular cartoon characters like Joe Camel to sell their cigarettes.

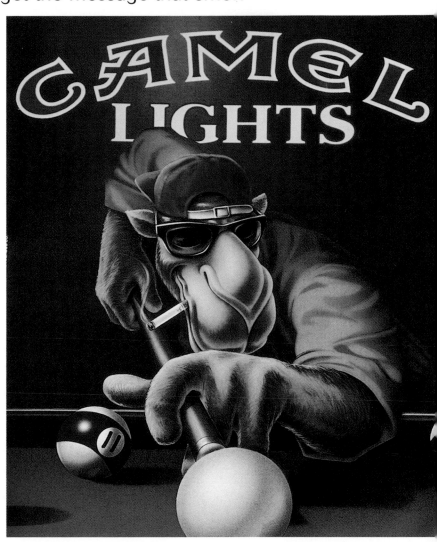

Cigarette advertisers have used cartoon characters to make smoking look cool to kids.

Activity 2: Who Do You Know Who Smokes?

Using this questionnaire, you can interview family and friends to find out who smokes and who doesn't. For those who smoke, you can learn how smoking affects their lives. For those who don't smoke, you can learn the reasons why.

1. How old are you?

2. Do you smoke?

3. Do you have any health problems? If so, what kind?

For people who say no to #2, answer questions 4-6

4. Did you ever smoke?

5. If not, why didn't you start?

6. If you used to smoke, when and why did you quit?

Smokers should answer questions 7-10

7. When did you start smoking?

8. Why did you start smoking? Did you hang out with friends who smoked?

9. Have you ever tried to quit smoking?

10. Why are you still smoking if you know that smoking can cause health problems?

Studies found that many kids knew all there was to know about Joe Camel. After years of angry complaints from parents and health officials, Joe Camel can no longer be used in cigarette ads.

Why would tobacco companies try to get teenagers to smoke? Some people say that as adult smokers quit smoking or die, tobacco sales will go down. So tobacco companies need new customers—young people who will buy their products for years.

Did You Know...

About 90 percent of adult smokers started when they were teenagers.

It's Quitting Time

If a smoker really wants to stop smoking, it should be a piece of cake, right? Just throw out those cigarettes and don't give it a second thought. For most people, it's not that easy. Remember that tobacco contains nicotine, which is very addictive. People who smoke

Although throwing out a pack of cig- arettes is easy, breaking an addiction to nicotine can be very hard.

crave nicotine. If they don't get it, they will feel miserable. Therefore, many smokers have a very hard time stopping.

How can people quit smoking? Some people are able to go "cold turkey." That means they just stop and never smoke another cigarette. This is not an easy thing to do. People who quit smoking still crave nicotine. When they don't get it, they may become restless, jittery, and irritable. These feelings are really strong in the beginning, but they go away in time. In the meantime, the person may not be too much fun to be around.

Many smokers can't quit cold turkey. They need to do it more gradually to avoid the unpleasant withdrawal symptoms. There are various products that can help people quit smoking. For example, a nicotine patch placed on a smoker's arm releases nicotine into the body through the skin. The person receives smaller and smaller amounts of nicotine over a period of several

Did You Know...

Most "quitters" have tried to stop smoking or chewing tobacco at least two or three times before they were able to give it up for good.

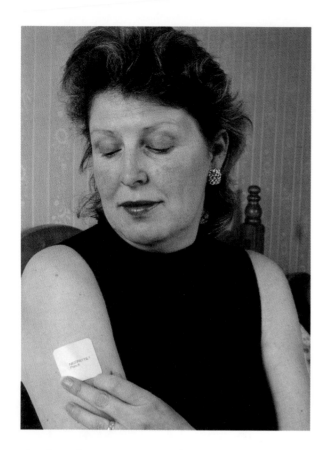

A nicotine patch can help smokers slowly reduce the nicotine they need.

weeks, until the body no longer needs the drug. This gradual process helps to reduce withdrawal symptoms.

Nicotine gum, which releases nicotine into a person's body through the lining of the mouth, works in much the same way as the nicotine patch. There are also pills that can be prescribed by a health care provider to help people quit smoking. People need to be careful when they use these products. Someone who chews too much of the gum—more than what the package says—may be putting too much nicotine into the body. This is no way to get over the addiction, and it could even be dangerous.

It's not just the addiction that makes it hard to quit smoking. Smoking is part of a smoker's daily routine, in the same way that in your routine, you brush your teeth first thing in the morning and before you go to bed at night. For a smoker, being at a party or hanging out with friends doesn't feel right without a cigarette. Someone trying to quit smoking must form new habits to break the connection with cigarettes. People need to find other things to do to keep their mouths and fingers busy. One way to do that is to chew gum or doodle with a pencil. (Some ex-smokers even chew pencils, which is not a good idea.) Some smokers like to light up after a meal. Sucking on a hard candy instead of smoking a cigarette is a way to keep the mouth busy.

There are a number of other tips and tricks that can help you or someone you know quit smoking. Exercise is a great way to get your mind off cigarettes. Every time you move, you are exercising your body. Exercise can be something you like to do, such as bike riding, playing soccer, or even walking the dog. Exercise also helps to make you feel good about yourself.

It is also important to drink lots of fluids. Water, juices, and caffeine-free sodas can help to wash nicotine out of the body. Stay away from sodas with caffeine, though. Caffeine tends to increase the desire to smoke. If you feel the urge to smoke, try breathing in and out, very slowly.

Did You Know....

Some people use food to replace smoking and then gain weight. However, the average smoker gains only 5 pounds (2.25 kilograms) after quitting. This small weight increase is still much healthier than smoking.

When you are done, drink a glass of water. This should help ease the craving.

Quitting smoking is something you do one day at a time. It can help if you reward yourself at the end of a day without smoking by doing something you enjoy, such as going to the movies or playing a game with friends.

Another helpful trick to keep yourself away from cig-arettes is thinking about all the bad things related to smoking. For example, picture a smoker's yellow teeth, bad breath, or blackened lungs. Think about how much healthier you will be if you don't smoke. You will have fewer colds, and you will be able to breathe more easily.

On the Road to Good Health

The American Cancer Society says that a smoker's health improves steadily after he or she quits.

1. After twenty minutes: Blood pressure starts to drop. Body temperature and pulse rate return to normal.
2. After eight hours: The carbon monoxide level in the blood decreases, and the amount of oxygen comes back to normal.
3. After twenty-four hours: The chance of heart attack is reduced.
4. After forty-eight hours: The ability to smell and taste improves.
5. After three days: Breathing is easier.
6. Within two to three months: Blood circulation improves. **Lung capacity** increases.
7. Within one to nine months: Shortness of breath decreases. Cilia start to grow back. Overall energy increases.
8. After one year: The risk of heart disease is half that of a smoker.
9. After five years: The risk of cancer of the mouth, throat, and esophagus is half that of a smoker, and the risk for lung cancer is reduced by almost half.
10. After ten years: The chances of lung cancer are about the same as those of a nonsmoker.

Smoking is not only bad for your health, it is also a very expensive habit. Lawmakers have put a heavy tax on cigarettes and other tobacco products, in hopes of getting people to quit. New laws are also helping fight against smoking. In many states, it is illegal to sell cigarettes to anyone under the age of eighteen. In a growing number of communities, cigarette vending machines can no longer be placed where young people can use them, and public places such as restaurants, business offices, shopping malls, and airports are now smoke-free.

Meanwhile, anti-smoking groups are working hard to educate the public about the dangers of smoking. Most of their efforts are aimed at teenagers, because most adult smokers first started to smoke when they were young. So if you don't want a lifetime of health problems, just say NO to cigarettes!

Anti-smoking groups create advertisements to warn people of the dangers of smoking.

Glossary

addictive—habit-forming; causing a person to depend on regular doses of a substance to feel good and avoid withdrawal symptoms

alveoli (sing. **alveolus**)—the tiny air sacs in the lungs, where gas exchange takes place

artery (pl. **arteries**)—a blood vessel that carries blood away from the heart to any part of the body

asthma—a disease in which the airways in the lungs become inflamed, making breathing difficult

blood clot—a jellylike solid formed by blood

blood vessel—a tube that carries blood from one part of the body to another

bronchi (sing. **bronchus**)—the larger air tubes of the lungs

bronchitis—inflammation of the bronchi

bronchioles—smaller air tubes of the lungs, which branch off from the bronchi

cholesterol—a fatty substance found in animals' bodies

cilia—tiny hairlike structures in the lining of the airways that move back and forth, sweeping foreign particles out and up to the throat

contract—to shorten

constrict—to narrow

crave—to feel a strong need for something

emphysema—a serious lung condition in which breathing is difficult due to damage to the tiny air bags in the lungs

exhale—to force air out of lungs

inflammation—redness and swelling as a result of damage or an allergic reaction

inhale—to breathe air into the lungs

lungs—two baglike organs used for breathing

lung capacity—the amount of air the lungs can hold after inhaling

muscles—strong, elastic tissues that pull on bones or other structures and move body parts

mucus—a gooey liquid produced by cells in the lining of the nose and breathing passages nicotine—a poisonous drug found in tobacco

pharynx—throat

platelets—tiny blood cells that help blood to clot

respiratory system—the organs involved in breathing, from the nose to the lungs

secondhand smoke—breathing in smoke produced when someone else smokes tobacco

stroke—a serious condition in which a person may lose the ability to speak or move a body part

tobacco—a plant whose leaves are used as the main ingredient in such products as cigarettes, cigars, and pipes

trachea—the windpipe; breathing tube that connects the nose to the bronchi

trigger—a substance or condition (such as dust or smoke) that brings on an asthma attack

tumor—a solid mass formed by a buildup of cancer cells

withdrawal symptoms—unpleasant or painful physical or emotional feelings that result from stopping the use of an addictive substance

Learning More

Books

Dodds, Bill. *1440 Reasons to Quit Smoking*. New York: Meadowbrook Press, 2000.

Gosselin, Kim. *Smoking Stinks!* Valley Park, MO: Jaylo Books, LLC, 1998.

Hyde, Margaret O. *Know About Smoking*. New York: Walker and Company, 1995.

Lang, Susan S. and Beth H. Marks. *Teens & Tobacco: A Fatal Attraction*. Brookfield, CT: Twenty-First Century Books, 1996.

Moe, Barbara. *Teen Smoking and Tobacco Use*. Berkeley Heights, NJ: Enslow Publishers, 2000.

Pietrusza, David. *Smoking*. San Diego, CA: Lucent Books, Inc., 1997.

Tobias, Andrew. *Kids Say Don't Smoke*. New York: Workman Publishing, 1991.

Williams, Mary E., ed. *Teen Smoking*. San Diego, CA: Greenhaven Press, Inc., 2000.

American Cancer Society
1599 Clifton Road, NE
Atlanta, GA 30329
404-320-3333
http://www.cancer.org/

American Lung Association
1740 Broadway
New York, NY 10019
http://www.lungusa.org/tobacco/

Great American Smokeout
*http://www.cancer.org/eprise/main/docroot/PED/ped_10_4?
sitearea=PED*
Background on the annual quit-smoking day and tips on how
to quit.

Smoking
http://kidshealth.org
Just type in Smoking to search the website for related articles.
Includes many kid-friendly links to articles about smoking.

Tobacco Information and Prevention Source (TIPS)
http://www.cdc.gov/tobacco/
Links to kid-friendly articles, a Kids Magazine, celebrities' views
on smoking, and fun free stuff.

Index

About the Authors

Dr. Alvin Silverstein is a professor of biology at the College of Staten Island of the City University of New York. **Virginia B. Silverstein** is a translator of Russian scientific literature. The Silversteins first worked together on a research project at the University of Pennsylvania. Since then, they have produced 6 children and more than 180 published books for young people.

Laura Silverstein Nunn, a graduate of Kean College, has been helping with her parents' books since her high-school days. She is the coauthor of more than 50 books on diseases and health, science concepts, endangered species, and pets. Laura lives with her husband, Matt, and their young son, Cory, in a rural New Jersey town not far from her childhood home.